T0199076

The Adventures of
Mason the Canning Jar

Bonnie Ramsey

Gena Pense

Sheila Sachs

Illustrated by Ramsey McWilliams

WestBow Press books may be ordered through booksellers or by contacting:

WestBow Press
A Division of Thomas Nelson & Zondervan
1663 Liberty Drive
Bloomington, IN 47403
www.westbowpress.com
844-714-3454

Interior Image Credit: Ramsey McWilliams

ISBN: 979-8-3850-0565-9 (sc)
ISBN: 979-8-3850-0566-6 (e)

Library of Congress Control Number: 2023916262

Print information available on the last page.

WestBow Press rev. date: 09/08/2023

WESTBOW
PRESS®
A DIVISION OF THOMAS NELSON
& ZONDERVAN

To our mom who taught us the love
for life that we now enjoy.

And the Lord God took the man, and put
him into the garden of Eden to dress it
and to keep it. Genesis 2:15 KJV

The Adventures of
Mason the Canning Jar

Hi, I'm Mason. I'm a canning jar.

I wonder what my job will be this summer?

I live in the garden shed in the winter, but in the summer I am filled with mouthwatering vegetables!

I look out the shed window and see many different tasty vegetables growing in the garden.

Soon they will be ready for harvesting.

When the vegetables are ready to harvest,
Grandma, my owner, will gather them.

Some vegetables will be cooked and served, but some of the extra vegetables will be put in a jar, like me. This is what I am used for.

Grandma uses me every summer for keeping
different kinds of vegetables to be eaten later.

One summer I held juicy red tomatoes. Everyone said I looked so pretty. The next summer Grandma canned cucumbers, and that made pickles!

My job isn't an easy one. I first have to be washed and dried and then, I have to get very hot before Grandma loads me up! The vegetables have to be very hot too. This is to make sure the vegetables are safe to be eaten later.

I think the best summer of all was when Grandma filled
me with her favorite thing to preserve, vegetable
soup! That has many delicious veggies in it.

Later in the summer, Grandma's neighbor got very sick. Filled with yummy, colorful soup, Grandma took me to her neighbor hoping to make her feel better.

The flavorful vegetable soup was cooked and just as Grandma had hoped, her neighbor got better!

Later, the neighbor washed me and gave me
back to Grandma with a thank you note.

After each adventure I am returned to the garden shed
to wait for the next summer. This is what makes me
special. I am filled with a new vegetable every summer!

I have been used for many years and will be used for
many more years. Grandma loves having good food
to feed her family and neighbors all winter long!

About the Author

As authors of this book, and sisters, we grew up with parents that survived the depression. They taught us to love God, love each other and love our communities. We all also share a love for educating children. We all three have served in or are serving in the public and private education system.

Realizing the art of canning is slowly becoming extinct we wanted to share these life experiences and knowledge with future generations. We watched our mom preserve food every summer throughout our lives. Our dad contributed by plowing, tilling and planting the vegetables we enjoyed then and for months to follow.

About the Illustrator

As illustrator of this book I would like to share something I feel is special. I was diagnosed with periventricular leukomalacia (PVL) and autism early in life and it caused me to be developmentally delayed. This diagnosis has not stopped me from doing what I love and being successful. My special interests are Disney, Chuck E. Cheese, kid shows, mascots and art. I've been so grateful to find employment that loves me for who I am and lets me use my unique skills. I am also blessed to have had connections with wonderful people over the years. Being autistic and delayed can be challenging sometimes, but I am an overcomer!

Printed in the United States
by Baker & Taylor Publisher Services